reading and
note-making

. . .

jeanne godfrey

Blackwell's/Palgrave Study Guides

Academic Writing
Being Critical
Reading and Note-making
Referencing
Study Skills A–Z
Writing Essays

Pocket Study Skills

14 Days to Exam Success
Brilliant Writing Tips for Students
Completing Your PhD
Doing Research
Getting Critical
Planning Your Dissertation
Planning Your Essay
Planning Your PhD
Posters and Presentations
Reading and Making Notes
Referencing and Understanding Plagiarism
Reflective Writing
Report Writing
Science Study Skills
Studying with Dyslexia
Success in Groupwork
Time Management
Writing for University

For a complete listing of all **Palgrave Study Skills** titles, please visit:
www.palgrave.com/studyskills

Contents

introduction

This short guide contains information, examples and tips on the essential aspects of reading and making notes for academic study and shows you the 'why' and 'how' of effective and successful reading and note-making.

Many of the themes covered in this guide are developed in the *Palgrave Study Skills* and *Pocket Study Skills* series, so these may be your next step for more detailed advice. Specific links are suggested at the bottom of the relevant pages throughout this guide.

1 Active reading and note-making

At university your tutors will expect you to decide for yourself which books, chapters and articles (often referred to as 'texts' or 'sources') are the most relevant for a particular course or assignment. Your tutors will also expect you to go beyond understanding what you read and to form views on whether the information is important, why, and how it relates to other information and ideas. Indeed, the whole point of academic study is to develop an active, critical approach to your material.

**Develop an active approach to reading –
engage with, think about and question what
you read:**

check that
you understand
accurately what the text says

break down and analyse the
ideas in detail

check for gaps, bias, unreliable
evidence or weak arguments

consider the ideas and information
given from different viewpoints

look for new connections or patterns with
information and ideas from other sources

reflect on and re-read the text to come
to your own unique understanding
and informed viewpoint

2 Purposeful reading and note-making

Before you start reading and making notes, decide
why you are going to do so. Having a clear purpose
is part of an active approach and will significantly
increase your level of engagement, criticality and
effectiveness. You will need to read for many
different purposes, some of which are listed
below. All these purposes are important aspects of
understanding and engaging with your discipline.

For more information on active and critical reading,
see *Critical thinking skills* and *Getting critical*.

Examples of different reading purposes	Examples of relevant source types
To widen your knowledge on a topic or issue	Course textbooks and sources on your reading list marked 'essential' or 'introductory'
To understand a subject-specific term	Introductory textbooks (these will usually have an explanatory glossary at the back) Subject-specific dictionaries
To learn about different perspectives on an issue	Academic journal articles
To find evidence that supports your own argument	Any relevant academic source
To check the accuracy of a specific fact given in a secondary source	The primary (original) source of the information
As preparation or follow-up to a seminar or lecture	Material specified by your tutor, lecture handouts, your own notes, more general sources on the seminar or lecture topic
For interest and enjoyment	Online articles, discussion boards, magazines, public interest books, relevant novels …

Examples of different note-making purposes

Before you start reading

- to brainstorm, predict and ask yourself questions about the topic and the text
- to write down what questions you want to address when you read.

While you are reading

to record key points

to note down reference details of sources mentioned in the text or in the list of references.

before, during or after reading

to summarise your own understanding of key points

to note down how the text relates to your own knowledge and experience

to collect points and ideas that can help develop your own argument and assignment

to note down ideas for your own research

to write down your questions and challenges to what the text says

to note things you want to investigate further

to note down useful and/or unknown words and phrases.

After reading

to write your own summary and reflection in your own words

to note down how you think information and ideas from other sources connect to or contrast with the text

to write down your own thoughts and ideas that have developed through reading the text.

For more guidance see *Reading and making notes*.

reading

3 Select your sources with care

A course reading list can be daunting, but you aren'
usually meant to read everything on it. Your tutor
wants to see that you can discriminate between the
different texts listed and find only those that are
directly relevant for a particular purpose.

If you are finding your own sources you need
to make sure that they are relevant and reliable.
Reliable sources are those that contain information
that is fair and correct according to context. For
example, if you needed to find out national public
opinion about a controversial topic, online social
media, and TV and radio chat shows would be a
reliable source of such data. For much academic
work, however, reliable sources are those that are
'academic' or 'scholarly'. These are texts written by
experts in the subject which have been reviewed by
other specialists before publication (a process called
peer review). When you are searching for your own
academic sources, particularly online, always check
to see whether they have been peer reviewed.

Other things to check for are:

• **Authorship.** Anonymous sources are more likely
  to be of poor quality and/or contain incorrect
  information. Be particularly careful with online
  material – remember, if you don't know who
  wrote something, you can't use it.

- **Date of publication.** Find the most current information and research on the topic, although you may also need to use older sources.
- **Accuracy.** Try to find the original (primary) source of information if possible, as something reported second or third hand may be less accurate and reliable. In reality you will often use secondary sources but you will usually also be expected to read the key primary texts on a topic.

Let's look at some sources a student found for an essay titled '*What rights do children in the UK have in terms of how they are portrayed in the media, and are these rights effective?*'.

The right-hand column contains brief comments on whether each source is likely to be relevant and reliable.

Source	Relevant and reliable?
Esmaeili M (2010). Children's rights and the media. *Journal of Family Research*. 6(1) pp115–129.	Yes, as long as it refers to the issue in the UK.
Covell K and Howe RB (2007). *Empowering children: Children's rights education as a pathway to citizenship.* Toronto: University of Toronto Press.	No. It is about educating children about their rights (probably in Canada, not the UK).
Children Now – media's impact. www.childrennow. org/index.php/learn/ medias_impact/	Might be relevant, depending on whether the article discusses children's rights. Might be reliable but you would need to find out more about 'Children Now'.

For more information on selecting and using sources, see *How to use your reading in your essays* pp5–9 and *Reading and making notes* pp25–45.

4 Read strategically

You are not expected to read everything in detail from start to finish – you need to develop the skill of matching the *way* you read something to *why* you are reading it.

There are three main ways of reading:

- **Scanning.** This is when you look over material quite quickly in order to pick out specific information.
- **Reading for gist** (also called 'skimming' or 'reading for breadth'). This is when you read something fairly quickly in order to understand the general idea and/or tone of the text.
- **Close reading** (also called 'reading in depth'). This is when you read a text or section of text in detail.

It is important to remember that scanning or reading for gist is *not* a substitute for close reading. You will need to do a lot of detailed reading for academic work, and one reason for only scanning or gist reading some texts is to give you enough time for careful and close reading of others.

5 Understand fully and accurately

When you read a text or section in detail, make sure that you have understood it *fully* and *accurately*. Below are some tips for helping you to do this.

1 Use the clues given by how the text is organised

Read the headings and sub-headings and reflect on what they say about the author's message. Look at the way sections are numbered, as this indicates how the author has grouped or separated their various points.

2 Read the text in an effective order

Read the introduction and conclusion and then read the first line of each paragraph to get the general idea of the author's message. Finally, go back and read the text in more detail.

3 Be clear on what different parts of the text are doing

To understand a text properly, you need to be able to distinguish between description, explanation, argument and opinion. Below are brief definitions of these functions, with examples from a student essay on children's rights in the UK.

- **Description**: Describes something but does *not* give reasons and does *not* try to judge or persuade the reader of something.

  Example:

  > A report published last year (CRAE 2013) stated that children's rights in the UK do not fully meet the requirements of the UN Convention on the Rights of the Child.

- **Explanation**: *Does* give reasons for something (and may also give a conclusion) but does *not* try to judge or persuade the reader of something.

  Example:

  > This is because there is still inconsistency in the application of some human rights, such as the low age of criminal responsibility and the fact that corporal punishment is still legal.

- **Argument**: An argument proposes a statement *and* gives reasons and evidence that lead to a particular conclusion *and* uses these reasons and conclusion to persuade the reader of an idea or action.

Below is an example of just the concluding sentences to the student's argument.

> The evidence given above shows that children in the UK not only do not have adequate legal rights but that they are unable to uphold the rights they do have. This needs to be redressed as a matter of urgency.

- **Opinion, agreement and disagreement**: Opinion, agreement and disagreement are points of view (perhaps, but not necessarily trying to persuade) *without* supporting evidence or logical reasoning. Opinion and dis/agreement are *not* valid arguments and in an academic text should only be given in addition to a properly supported argument, not instead of one.

An example of an opinion would be:

> I think that children in the UK should be given more legal rights.

4 Use clues given in the language of the text

- Look out for language 'signposts' which tell you that a main point, change or section is coming up.

  Examples:
  - *There are three main problems … First, … second, … finally, …*
  - *The question / issue is …*
  - *The main cause / effect is …*
  - *Importantly, …*

- Look at the verbs authors use, as these tell you what the author is doing.

  Examples:
  - *I suggest / I propose / I argue* – author is setting out their argument
  - *This illustrates / indicates / establishes* – author is giving supporting evidence or ideas
  - *This fails to / neglects / overlooks* – author is criticising opposing evidence or ideas.

- Be aware of how authors use signposts such as *X strongly suggests* / *X may indicate* / *X might possibly mean that* to indicate how sure or unsure they are about their claim.

- Check that you are clear on the meaning of words that link sentences or parts of a sentence, e.g. *however* / *nevertheless* / *despite* / *although* / *whereas* / *moreover* / *also* / *in addition*.

- Be clear what the author is referring to when they use words such as *this* / *that* / *they* / *which* / *such*.

- Check your understanding of noun groups (e.g. *the Western anti-climate change position* or *a vulnerability anti-virus update scan*) which are common in academic texts.

5 Avoid these common reading pitfalls

- **Misinterpreting the main point of data**
  Try to first understand the overall key message of any data rather than getting lost in the details. Once you have understood the main point, you can go back and analyse the data more carefully.

- **Not noticing degree or frequency**
  For example, there is a big difference between the statements 'children's rights do not meet the requirements' and 'children's rights do not fully meet the requirements'.

  Notice also the difference between comparative phrases and superlatives. It is one thing to say that 'children's rights in the UK are worse than …' and another to say that 'children's rights in the UK are the worst'.

- **Overlooking *not* or *no***
  Pay attention to the words *not*, *no* and other phrases that indicate a negative. Overlooking these may mean that you accidentally reverse the author's meaning.

- **Misinterpreting who says what**
  For example, in our boxed examples on page 8, it is not the student who is stating that UK children's rights do not fully meet the requirements of the UN Convention, but the CRAE report.
- **Guessing or ignoring words you don't understand**
  If you aren't sure what a word means, look it up.

6 Analyse, evaluate and create new knowledge

Look again at the section on p2 to remind yourself of the essential points on active reading. Although you need to understand what the author is saying on the page, you also need to go beyond this level of understanding and decide what *you* think about the author's message.

Analyse

Break down and examine each concept and definition the author gives.

Are these definitions accurate or are there borderline cases where the author's definitions might not apply?

Are there other ways in which the concepts could be defined and if so, how does this affect the author's argument?

What assumptions does the author make and are these assumptions valid?

Does the author's set of reasons link logically to their conclusion or are there flaws or gaps in the argument?

Evaluate

Who is the author and who do they work for?

What has the author tried to do and are they successful?

What is the author's perspective and general way of thinking?

Is the author's supporting evidence reliable, objective and relevant to their argument?

Do you think the text is important and why/why not?

Do you think other people will read the text and if so, who might these people be and why might they read it?

Create new knowledge

Can you use your analysis and evaluation to see new ways of grouping or contrasting the concepts and ideas?

Can you use your insights to develop new perspectives, conclusions or solutions?

For more on understanding and evaluating what you read, see *How to use your reading in your essays* pp17–23 and *Reading and making notes* pp65–95.

making notes

7 Make notes because …

If you don't usually make notes, consider the advantages of doing so:

- helps you to concentrate on what you are reading
- keeps you motivated by tracking and signalling reading progress
- starts you on the process of using your own words and style
- gives you your own unique record of the text
- helps you to reflect on and make connections between different pieces of knowledge, leading to a better understanding of your subject
- as a result of all the above, usually leads to higher marks.

8 Ensure your notes are effective

Have a clear purpose

Think about what function you want your notes to perform. For example, do you want them to help you:

- extract all the essential points and arguments?
- note down only information on a specific theme?
- clarify how points relate to each other and see how the ideas are organised?

Whatever the purpose of your notes and whatever form they take (linear, diagrams, drawings), they should be fairly brief while still making sense to you and providing you with the information you need.

Key features of effective notes	Why is this important?
Full reference details, including the relevant page numbers.	You will only be able to use your notes in your assignment if you can give full reference details. These are also useful if you need to find the source again later.
Information on when/where you made the notes.	This will help you keep track of your research over time.
Your purpose and questions written at the top of your notes.	To keep your notes focused and help stop you making notes that you don't need and will never use. If you find that you need more information at a later date, you can always go back to the text.
Information that is not *too detailed* or *too brief*.	If your notes are too detailed it might be because you are copying whole sentences or sections from the text. However, if your notes are too brief, the meaning will be unclear and you won't understand them when you re-read them.
Clear distinction between main and minor points, and between points and examples.	If you find you can't separate out the main points, it might be because you don't really understand the text. Think about whether you even need to make notes on minor points.

A clear system for showing which parts of your notes are:	
• exact phrases/ sentences from the text (quotations);	You must keep careful track of quotations (even very short ones) in your notes to make sure that you reference them in your final assignment – use colour, quotation marks or write them in a separate space.
• *mostly* the same words from the text, or a mixture of your words and those from the text (close paraphrase);	Again, you need to keep a careful track of this because for your assignment you will need to rewrite these bits so that they are completely or almost completely (90%) in your own words.
• your *own* words to describe information from the text (paraphrase);	Do try to use your own words in your notes. You may be worried about changing the meaning of the text accidentally or not being able to express things well, but your confidence in using your own words will increase with practice. Make sure you also note down when the author of the text cites *other* authors so that you attribute the information to the right person.
• your own comments, questions and summaries;	It's a good idea to have a separate column or space for these.
• legibility.	Notes do not have to be particularly neat but you do need to be able to read them.
A key to the abbreviations you have used.	Using abbreviations will help prevent copying and will encourage you to use your own style, but keep a record of what key abbreviations mean.
White space.	In case you need to add anything later.

Below is a source extract followed by some effective notes. Notice that in their notes the student has written their questions and predictions at the top and has used a separate column for their own comments. Notice also that the student has used mainly their own words and has put any copied phrases, words and even statistics in quotation marks.

Source extract

How the UK is doing on children's rights

74% of those in the survey thought that the UK is 'good' or 'very good' at making sure children are given their rights.

20% thought the UK is 'just OK'.

6% thought the UK is 'bad' or 'very bad' at making sure children are given their rights.

60% thought the UK is getting better at making sure children are given their rights, 31% weren't sure, and 10% thought the UK is getting worse at making sure children are given their rights.

Differences of more than 5 percentage points in how different groups thought the UK is doing on children's rights were:

Children under 14 were more likely than those over 14 to rate the UK as being 'good' or 'very good' at making sure children are given their rights. 78% of under 14s rated the UK this way, compared with 71% of those aged 14 and over.

Children in care were less likely than other children to rate the UK as being 'good' or 'very good' at making sure children are given their rights. 69% of children in care rated the UK as good or very good, compared with 74% of children generally.

Among children in care, foster children were more likely than those in children's homes to rate the UK as being 'good' or 'very good' at making sure children are given their rights.

Extract from: *The United Nations Committee on the Rights of the Child: How children say the UK is doing.* 15 July 2014. p.30 www.gov.uk/government/publications [Accessed on 30/3/2015]

Student notes

My Qs. – How do children in the UK feel about children's rights? Problems and issues?

Predictions – Children don't know about their rights and that the main problem areas are around the right to a good standard of living and personal safety

30/03/2015

The United Nations Committee on the Rights of the Child: How children say the UK is doing. 15 July 2014. p.30 www.gov.uk/government/publications. Found by searching the gov.uk website for 'children's rights'.

My comments	Info from p30
Are the children in the survey from all social groups? How many? Ages? Regions? Me to read the intro. and look at the end refs.	Children were asked the question 'How is the UK doing on children's rights'.
Better than I thought!	Over 70% thought UK was 'good' or 'very good' at children being given their rights.
NB = Combined 40% didn't think UK is getting better.	'60%' thought UK is 'getting better' at giving children their rights, 31% not sure and 10% said 'getting worse'.
Interesting – why is this? – investigate further?	Small decrease in 'good'/'very good' rating in gp. over age 14.
Not surprising – I would have expected bigger diff.	Childn. in care were 5% less happy about rights than general population and within the care cat. childn. in homes were less happy about rights than those with foster parents.
Report doesn't give the percentage difference for this – why?	

Main flaw in survey –
**how fairly can younger
children assess
whether they are
being given their
rights?**

9   Consider different note-making formats

You probably already use a particular note-making format, but you might find it useful to experiment with some new ones so that you can vary your format according to your purpose and the type of material from which you are making notes.

Linear or list notes

Linear notes are written out in lines using lists, bullet points or numbering. They are an easy format to type and are good for distinguishing between major and minor points and examples. Linear notes are handy if the information is fairly ordered and has particular stages or groupings. It's a good idea to start each new point on a new line and to use indentation and spacing to show how information groups together. Don't forget to leave white space somewhere on the page for adding things later.

Cornell or 'split page' notes

These are linear-style notes with a left-hand column for your own comments and ideas, plus a space for your own summary at the bottom. The notes on pages 18 and 19 are an example of this split page format.

_____

For more on effective note-making, see *Reading and making notes* Chs 20, 21 and 22 and *The study skills handbook* Ch 6.

Paragraph notes

This is when you read/listen without making notes and then write a paragraph summary afterwards. These are good for expressing the key points of the information in your own words and for helping you process and understand the text. One disadvantage of summary paragraph notes is that you probably won't be able to remember details or large amounts of information.

Pattern or visual notes

Pattern (also called visual) notes often have the key idea in the middle with other information branching off and so are also sometimes called nuclear notes or spidergrams. Pattern notes can help you remember information and are good for noting down the overall structure of someone's argument and for seeing connections between things.

If you use pattern notes, make sure that they still have the essential features listed on pages 15 and 16.

Flowcharts

Notes in the form of a flowchart are useful if the text involves sequences and processes.

Table notes

Using tables can be useful for topics and information that have several different strands or similar aspects that you want to compare, for looking at two sides of an argument and for noting the advantages and disadvantages of something. For example, you can use a table to note down different authors' viewpoints on a particular issue.

Mind maps

Mind maps are used to brainstorm your *own* ideas and thoughts either before you read or to help see connections between sources after reading. Mind maps are also commonly used to brainstorm content and structure for an assignment.

For more on different note-making formats, see *Reading and making notes* Ch 23.

10   Get the most from lectures and audio-visual material

Before

Do the reading or other preparation your tutor/ lecturer asks you to.

Check the module website regularly for last-minute changes, additional information or guidance.

Brainstorm what you already know about the topic, how it relates to past lectures and material and what your questions and ideas about it are – jot down some notes.

Read any handouts or slides available. You may like to download and print lecture PowerPoint (PPT) slides beforehand so that you can make notes on them during the lecture.

Make sure you understand key terms and vocabulary – this will make a huge difference to how much you understand during the lecture/material.

Prepare your note-making material and layout, leaving white space on your note paper so that you can correct and add things after the lecture.

If you have access to the PPT slides before the lecture, you can open them and make notes during the lecture in the *notes page* box under each slide (squash up each slide by moving up its bottom edge so that you have more room in the notes box).

During

For face-to-face lectures, arrive on time and have the right note-making materials ready. Sit towards the front of the lecture room – it's easy to become disengaged or distracted if you are sitting near the back.

If the lecturer gives a handout at the start of the lecture, you can make notes on this as you go along, but *don't* try to read it while the lecturer is speaking; prioritise listening and save reading the handout until afterwards.

Different lecturers will have different accents, styles and speeds, so don't panic if you find someone hard to understand. Relax and just listen for a while to familiarise yourself with their voice.

The lecturer will often start by outlining the structure of their content and the key points s/he will discuss, so *listen* to this without making any notes.

Listen out for when the lecturer emphasises important points by raising their voice or by speaking more slowly and repeating key messages. They may also use body language to emphasise points and pause to separate points.

Listen out for signpost language that will help you understand the structure, direction and key points of the lecture. For example:

- Words that indicate cause and effect: e.g. *consequently, because of this, as a result, this is due to*
- Words that indicate an important point is coming: e.g. *crucially, importantly, remember, especially*
- Words that qualify a statement: e.g. *always, sometimes, usually, generally, rarely, never, only*
- Words that indicate examples or supporting evidence: e.g. *such as, an illustration of this is, research / a study by x shows that*

Don't try to write everything down – leave time to really listen and understand what the lecturer is saying and capture the main messages. Just note the key points and briefly jot down your own comments.

Listen carefully towards the end of the lecture, when the lecturer might summarise the most important points.

If the lecturer refers to a source, note this down and find the full reference after the lecture.

In a face-to-face lecture you can often politely ask the lecturer to repeat or clarify something.

Remember that you don't have to make notes. You might find it more useful to prepare well beforehand, listen carefully to the lecture and then make some notes immediately afterwards.

If you can't or don't want to make notes during a face-to-face lecture, record it and listen to it later, but ask the lecturer for permission to record.

After

Review and add to your notes to make sure that you can understand them. Underline key points, correct any errors, fill in points you missed and look up any words or terms you don't understand.

If you used the notes pages to add notes to a PPT lecture, you can review the presentation and delete any less important or irrelevant slides. You can then print out the slides and your notes by going to *print* and selecting *notes view* on the *print what?* menu.

You need to become a *critical* listener, that is, to ask yourself questions and evaluate what you have heard or seen. However, it is not always possible to listen/watch and to be critical at the same time, so critically reviewing the lecture or material as soon as possible afterwards is important. Analyse the lecture/material content and write down your own evaluation, ideas and questions. What follow-up questions would you like to ask? What further research and references do you want to chase up? How does the content relate to the rest of the module and your course in general? What really interested you?

If you have recorded a lecture, listen to it again as soon as possible and make notes and/or fill in any important gaps.

Follow up and get full reference details of any recommended reading, links and cross-references given by the lecturer. Check the module website for

_____

For more on making notes from lectures and audio-visual material, see *Reading and making notes* Ch 24.

these references and any other information posted after the lecture.

Discuss the lecture/material content with other students.

11 Rework your notes

Research shows that students who look back over their notes to check for clarity and meaning are more successful learners, and that the sooner you review your notes after taking them, the better. Research also shows that students who reflect on and rework their notes are more successful, so try some of these:

- Rewrite your notes using use a different format, for example, from linear to pattern notes or vice versa. This will help you review and reflect on what you have written down.
- Write a short summary – what would you say if a friend asked you to tell them about the book or lecture? This will help you to clarify your understanding, use your own words and improve retention of information.
- Use your notes to write a short critical reflection.
- Review your notes on the topic from previous weeks and look for connections and similarities or differences between different ideas, arguments, evidence and viewpoints.
- Reorganise your notes around your own unique question or angle to help develop your own 'voice'.
- If you have an assignment title, reorganise your notes around this, adding comments and identifying any knowledge gaps.

For more on making the most of your notes, see *Reading and making notes* Chs 26 and 27.

Look after your notes

You will need to refer back to your notes in the future, so keep them organised and safe from physical damage or loss.

Linked books in the *Palgrave Study Skills* and *Pocket Study Skills* series

Cottrell S (2011). *Critical thinking skills* (2nd edition). Basingstoke: Palgrave Macmillan.

Cottrell S (2013). *The study skills handbook* (4th edition). Basingstoke: Palgrave Macmillan.

Godfrey J (2013). *How to use your reading in your essays* (2nd edition). Basingstoke: Palgrave Macmillan.

Godfrey J (2014). *Reading and making notes* (2nd edition). Basingstoke: Palgrave Macmillan.

Godfrey J (2011). *Writing for university*. Basingstoke: Palgrave Macmillan.

Williams K (2014). *Getting critical* (2nd edition). Basingstoke: Palgrave Macmillan.

Williams K and Carroll J (2009). *Referencing and understanding plagiarism*. Basingstoke: Palgrave Macmillan.

POCKET STUDY SKILLS
Jeanne Godfrey
READING & MAKING NOTES
SECOND EDITION

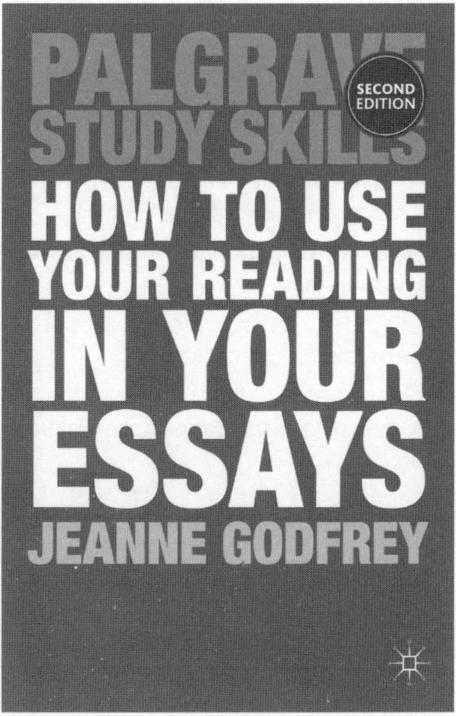
PALGRAVE STUDY SKILLS
SECOND EDITION
HOW TO USE YOUR READING IN YOUR ESSAYS
JEANNE GODFREY

First published 2015 by
PALGRAVE

Palgrave in the UK is an imprint of Macmillan Publishers Limited, registered in England, company number 785998, of 4 Crinan Street, London, N1 9XW.

Palgrave Macmillan in the US is a division of St Martin's Press LLC, 175 Fifth Avenue, New York, NY 10010.

Palgrave is a global imprint of the above companies and is represented throughout the world.

Palgrave® and Macmillan® are registered trademarks in the United States, the United Kingdom, Europe and other countries.

ISBN: 978-1-137-54050-8   paperback

This book is printed on paper suitable for recycling and made from fully managed and sustained forest sources. Logging, pulping and manufacturing processes are expected to conform to the environmental regulations of the country of origin.

A catalogue record for this book is available from the British Library.

A catalog record for this book is available from the Library of Congress.